Beyond the Resistance

Learning to Face Adversity

Foreword by Ian Leitch

Dave Wager

Grace Acres Press
P.O. Box 22
Larkspur, CO 80118
888-700-GRACE (4722)
(303) 681-9995
(303) 681-9996 fax
www.GraceAcresPress.com

Grace Acres Press also publishes books in a variety of
electronic formats. Some content that appears in print may
not be available in electronic books.

Scripture quotations marked NLT are taken from the
Holy Bible, New Living Translation, copyright © 1996, 2004.
Used by permission of Tyndale House Publishers, Inc.,
Wheaton, IL 60189. All rights reserved.

Library of Congress Cataloging-in-Publication Data:

ISBN-13: 978-1-60265-001-5
ISBN-10: 1-60265-001-2

Printed in the United States of America

10 09 08 07   01 02 03 04 05 06 07 08 09 10

This book is dedicated to the many who have gone before me who chose to be significant, who stood firm when others wilted, who charged the enemy while others fled. This book is also dedicated to my dad, Richard Wager, the ultimate intimate warrior for our King. His memory evokes a powerful desire to finish the fight to which God has called me.

Danger feared is folly, danger faced is freedom.

— V. Raymond Edman

Contents

About the Author

For the past twenty-five years, Dave Wager has served as a leader, friend, and teacher to thousands who have entered the educational grounds of Silver Birch Ranch in White Lake, Wisconsin. Today Dave continues to serve as the president of Silver Birch Ranch, and also teaches at camps, conferences, churches, and businesses throughout the world.

Dave's life has been dedicated to the growth of young people, first as a volunteer youth worker and then later as a fifth-grade teacher. He has served as president of the Wisconsin Christian Camping Association and currently teaches a class in "Christian Life and Ethics" at the Nicolet Bible Institute. Dave holds a B.A. from Wheaton College and an M.S. Ed. from Northern Illinois University.

Dave desires that each person he meets walk intimately with God and fulfill the purposes for which he or she was designed. He believes that joy and effectiveness in life, work, and ministry come from knowing what really matters. His focus is in examining how today's choices affect the real bottom line: knowing what we are about, what are our responsibilities, and what are God's responsibilities.

Foreword

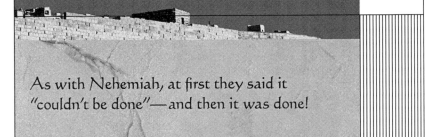

As with Nehemiah, at first they said it
"couldn't be done"—and then it was done!

I first met Dave Wager at Silver Birch Ranch in 1988:
a strong character, both physically and spiritually. Now
eighteen years on, he is still strong, albeit smoothed and
polished by his wife, two daughters, and the leadership
of Silver Birch Ranch.

The ranch has expanded to 100 acres and has about
50 buildings. The year-round retreats are as large as
the summer programs. The dream of having a one-year
college has been realized in the creation of Nicolet
Bible Institute, and the youth and family camps are
often filled to capacity. Wager's experience in working
toward these goals clearly shows in this book.

With this book, Wager proposes twenty-one thoughts
for those involved in leadership and building a ministry.
It is short, concise, and exactly on target. The character
of the man is all over the book: I write it, you read it
and grow up, man!

This is not a book for the weak-hearted. This is a book
for the bold and the brave. It is not a book for those
who want to maintain the status quo, but for those who
want to expand and develop their ministries. It is not
a book just to read, but for use to check motive, purpose,
and your very soul—so read it at your own risk!

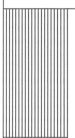

Thought for Day 1 starts the ball rolling: "The first step in any effective ministry is to have its leadership gripped by the obvious problems the leaders see, in a way that compels them into action." It flows from there into confession and repentance and on to, "As a leader, have I surrounded myself with people who have a compelling desire to honor God? How do I know?"

Wager's concern, desire, and character radiate from these pages. The thoughts for each day are razor-sharp and you can easily cut yourself on them: "Praying and working hard is the answer." "Expect the work to be harder than it should be." "You might need to ask your people for a ridiculous commitment." "Not only should I, as a leader, be willing to work for less than I deserve, I must be willing to expend my personal assets to see the work accomplished." "There will be people who blatantly lie about you." "Success with leadership and the people will always be proportionate to the spiritual sensitivity of people."

Wager writes for Christian leaders who truly want to hear and listen to God's thoughts on their ministry over a three-week period. If you read this honestly, with an open heart, you will never be the same again.

I'll let Dave Wager have the last word: "Whatever the task God has placed on your heart, He also has a plan. He is older than you, smarter than you, and loves you; you can trust Him."

IAN LEITCH
Edinburgh, Scotland
November 2006

Preface

While playing defensive end for the Wheaton College football team, I noticed that I was always in the middle of the play—in the middle of where I was supposed to be—whenever I ran into resistance. I also noticed that when there was no resistance—when I was left alone—I was either getting set up or totally out of the play. I learned early to recognize the resistance and turn into it. Each and every time I rushed the resistance, I was significant in the eventual outcome of that play.

I have found this principle to hold true in life as well. Where I encounter resistance, I usually find something going on that is significant in the Kingdom work. When I choose to rush this resistance, I choose to be a significant part of the eventual victory.

Acknowledgments

I would like to thank Coach John Swider and Coach DeWayne "Dewy" King for believing in what I could be rather than what I was, while firmly but gently teaching me about what lies beyond the resistance.

Introduction

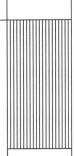

Many people are involved in nonprofit Christian organizations. In these positions, they encounter the many unique challenges of nonprofit leadership.

How do those who are Christian leaders differ from those who are not? Why do we operate nonprofits? What do we hope to get from our efforts?

The following thoughts were written for the Christian leader, pastor, lay leader, or corporate officer who would like to sit, think, and pray about what is next for the organization he or she leads. This three-week meditation guide is intended to facilitate just that, acting as a catalyst for meditation and prayer.

We suggest that before you start this study, you spend some time on your knees seeking God's heart for your organization. Then, read the book of Nehemiah through once or twice and try to pick out the principles that guided Nehemiah through turbulent days. After that, begin using this guide: read one entry a day for twenty-one days and spend an hour or so each day sipping coffee, staring out a window, and thinking about that entry. Ask God to give you the same guidance and results he gave Nehemiah.

Whatever the task God has placed on your heart, He also has a plan. He is older than you, smarter than you, and loves you; you can trust Him.

Thought for Day 1

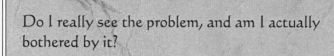

Do I really see the problem, and am I actually bothered by it?

NEHEMIAH 1:3–6 (NLT)

They said to me, "Things are not going well for those who returned to the province of Judah. They are in great trouble and disgrace. The wall of Jerusalem has been torn down, and the gates have been destroyed by fire."

4 When I heard this, I sat down and wept. In fact, for days I mourned, fasted, and prayed to the God of heaven.

5 Then I said, "O Lord, God of heaven, the great and awesome God who keeps his covenant of unfailing love with those who love him and obey his commands,

6 Listen to my prayer! Look down and see me praying night and day for your people Israel.

Nehemiah was not indifferent to the sin and disgrace that were brought to his attention. He did not shrug his spiritual shoulders and blame things on the world system, the religious system, or the media of his day. Instead, he sat down and wept. In fact, he wept for days; he mourned, he fasted, and he prayed.

Of notable interest is the fact that Nehemiah had a cushy job, as cupbearer to the king. This news did not directly affect Nehemiah's personal life; he could have ignored it and gone on enjoying the position that God had given him. The easy thing would have been to verbally condemn or rue what he had heard and then continue taking care of himself.

Or he could actually think about what he had heard and let it grip his soul. Nehemiah could begin to ask God why He had placed him where he was and why he had such good access to the king. He could begin to ask what he could do, if anything, to solve the problem.

The first step in any effective ministry is to have its leadership gripped by the obvious problems the leaders see, in a way that compels them into action.

So, what is the problem that God would have you observe? Have you dismissed the problem, or are you allowing God's Holy Spirit to bother you with a holy sorrow? What position or resources has God given you that He might use to solve the problem? Would you be willing to get involved if it meant giving up a secure position, giving up personal resources, working with ingrates, and doing battle with Satan himself?

Nehemiah was one who allowed himself to get gripped by the problem. He allowed himself to look at it, struggle with it, and dream about what could be done.

This is always step one.

I need to ask God to help me see the real problem—and once I see it, please help me honestly address it!

Beyond the Resistance: Learning to Face Adversity

Thought for Day 2

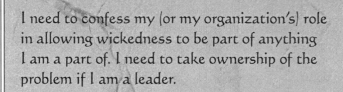

I need to confess my (or my organization's) role in allowing wickedness to be part of anything I am a part of. I need to take ownership of the problem if I am a leader.

NEHEMIAH 1:6–8 (NLT)

6 . . . I CONFESS THAT WE HAVE SINNED AGAINST YOU. YES, EVEN MY OWN FAMILY AND I HAVE SINNED!

7 WE HAVE SINNED TERRIBLY BY NOT OBEYING THE COMMANDS, DECREES, AND REGULATIONS THAT YOU GAVE US THROUGH YOUR SERVANT MOSES.

8 PLEASE REMEMBER WHAT YOU TOLD YOUR SERVANT MOSES: 'IF YOU ARE UNFAITHFUL TO ME, I WILL SCATTER YOU AMONG THE NATIONS . . . .'"

Confession is a normal part of a leader's life. Repentance is a normal part of any Christian's life. When there is no repentance, there is no blessing. As humans, we do things according to our own understanding, but we do not always do right. It is good to sit in the presence of the Almighty and admit that He has always been right and is right now. Nehemiah starts here, with a confession of his own and his people's sin.

Scripture contains many instances of leaders asking God to forgive their people. It all started with Job, who regularly sacrificed for his children, and at the end of his travails asked for forgiveness for his well-meaning but wrong friends. At the end of the book of Job, things got on track when Job, of all people, repented and accepted personal responsibility.

All leaders have some personal responsibility in the tragedies they are burdened with. Repentance is a powerful weapon against Satan that God has given us to use. As we wield this weapon, Satan trembles, for we are agreeing with God, depending on His mercy and grace and aligning ourselves with the One who cannot lose.

It is one thing to know of a problem. It is another to be bothered by the problem and to accept one's own part in the problem. This insight into Nehemiah's life helps us see the mindset of an effective leader.

A good leader is a good repenter. How are you doing in this area?

I need to approach God as God. I need to continually understand that His dumbest thought is infinitely greater than my smartest thought. I need to remember that I often do not understand, and that when I, or my people, are wrong, I need to confess our errors and sin, not sugar-coat or dismiss them.

1 JOHN 1:9 (NLT)

9 BUT IF WE CONFESS OUR SINS TO HIM, HE IS FAITHFUL AND JUST TO FORGIVE US OUR SINS AND TO CLEANSE US FROM ALL WICKEDNESS.

Thought for Day 3

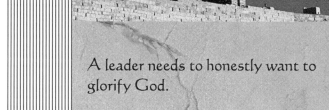

A leader needs to honestly want to glorify God.

NEHEMIAH 1:10–11 (NLT)

10 "THE PEOPLE YOU RESCUED BY YOUR GREAT POWER AND STRONG HAND ARE YOUR SERVANTS.

11 O LORD, PLEASE HEAR MY PRAYER! LISTEN TO THE PRAYERS OF THOSE OF US WHO DELIGHT IN HONORING YOU. PLEASE GRANT ME SUCCESS TODAY BY MAKING THE KING FAVORABLE TO ME. PUT IT INTO HIS HEART TO BE KIND TO ME." IN THOSE DAYS I WAS THE KING'S CUP-BEARER.

Observe Nehemiah's heart in this passage. He asks God to listen to his prayer and to all the prayers of those who delight in honoring Him.

Nehemiah knows that the goal in life is to glorify God. He knows that we were made to honor Him and he asks God to listen to this select group of people who have the same desire.

As a leader, have I surrounded myself with people who have a compelling desire to honor God? How do I know?

It is easy to get trapped in "stealth honoring," that is, putting myself in a position where my words say that I want to honor God, but I am hoping that enough people notice—well, honor *me*—so that I actually feel good about what I am doing. It is much more difficult to pray, and mean, what Elijah prayed: that when the miracle I am hoping for is accomplished, all those involved and all those who were on the fringes would know that God was indeed God and that I was just His servant.

I cannot count the number of times someone has shared good news and I wanted to tell them that I had been praying for them. This "announced" prayer may sound good to me and, I am certain, sounds good to the other person, yet in reality what I am trying to do is steal glory and honor from God and deflect a little my way. I would love to be recognized as being needed, even though I am not. I would love to get recognition as one who is vital to the mission, even though I am not.

Nehemiah recognizes that there is a group of people, a unique and holy group, who actually desire that God be honored. He asks God to heed those people's prayers.

If I were to ask God to answer only the prayers of those who actually wanted to honor Him, I wonder how many prayers of my staff, congregations, friends, and so on would be answered?

It is easy to look away on this issue. I need to ask myself what the real purposes of my prayers are. I need to ask God to help me actually see me as I am; He already sees me. I need to be bold enough to ask God to ignore the self-centered, self-indulgent, pride-filled prayers from me and my people.

BEYOND THE RESISTANCE: Learning to Face Adversity

Thought for Day 4

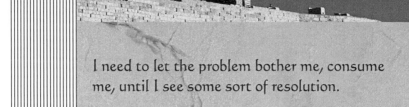

I need to let the problem bother me, consume me, until I see some sort of resolution.

NEHEMIAH 2:1–4 (NLT)

1 EARLY THE FOLLOWING SPRING, IN THE MONTH OF NISAN, DURING THE TWENTIETH YEAR OF KING ARTAXERXES' REIGN, I WAS SERVING THE KING HIS WINE. I HAD NEVER BEFORE APPEARED SAD IN HIS PRESENCE.

2 SO THE KING ASKED ME, "WHY ARE YOU LOOKING SO SAD? YOU DON'T LOOK SICK TO ME. YOU MUST BE DEEPLY TROUBLED." THEN I WAS TERRIFIED,

3 BUT I REPLIED, "LONG LIVE THE KING! HOW CAN I NOT BE SAD? FOR THE CITY WHERE MY ANCESTORS ARE BURIED IS IN RUINS, AND THE GATES HAVE BEEN DESTROYED BY FIRE."

4 THE KING ASKED, "WELL, HOW CAN I HELP YOU?" . . .

Many would say that I need to rest in the fact that God is sovereign. Indeed He is, and He does have a plan, and He can accomplish this plan with or without me.

That being a given, I also need to understand that for some reason God has chosen to use humans for His work. I can choose to remain indifferent to the spiritual war and the casualties around me and keep fattening myself unto the slaughter, or I can be consumed with the war, its purposes, and the role my King has for me.

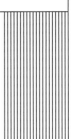

Nehemiah was consumed with the problem and stayed consumed until there was some resolution.

It was dangerous to be sad in front of the king. It was humanly silly for Nehemiah to allow himself to be continually bothered when he had such a good life that was not really affected by the events so far away. He could have started with a consuming passion, but let it dwindle and slip away over time by involving himself in other duties. By that time, he could have shrugged it off, "given it to God" to deal with, and gone about his business as usual.

For some reason, though, he chose not to. For some reason, Nehemiah chose to remain bothered. He chose to dwell on what must change—not on what was, but on what must change.

The king noticed Nehemiah's preoccupation with this gripping problem. That was a moment of testing for Nehemiah. He was supposed to carry out his duties as if the evil he knew about was not that bad. But he could not live that way, even though the problem did not directly affect his life.

So often, I am not only *not* troubled by the evil I see, I actually embrace it. So often it is easy to accommodate the evil in our lives, adjust to the evil, get used to the evil. Nehemiah did not and I should not. It should be obvious to all that I am bothered by evil and that I remain bothered by it until there is resolution.

BEYOND THE RESISTANCE: Learning to Face Adversity

Thought for Day 5

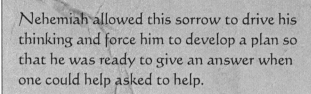

Nehemiah allowed this sorrow to drive his thinking and force him to develop a plan so that he was ready to give an answer when one could help asked to help.

NEHEMIAH 2:4–8 (NLT)

4 ... WITH A PRAYER TO THE GOD OF HEAVEN,

5 I REPLIED, "IF IT PLEASE THE KING, AND IF YOU ARE PLEASED WITH ME, YOUR SERVANT, SEND ME TO JUDAH TO REBUILD THE CITY WHERE MY ANCESTORS ARE BURIED."

6 THE KING, WITH THE QUEEN SITTING BESIDE HIM, ASKED, "HOW LONG WILL YOU BE GONE? WHEN WILL YOU RETURN?" AFTER I TOLD HIM HOW LONG I WOULD BE GONE, THE KING AGREED TO MY REQUEST.

7 I ALSO SAID TO THE KING, "IF IT PLEASE THE KING, LET ME HAVE LETTERS ADDRESSED TO THE GOVERNORS OF THE PROVINCE WEST OF THE EUPHRATES RIVER, INSTRUCTING THEM TO LET ME TRAVEL SAFELY THROUGH THEIR TERRITORIES ON MY WAY TO JUDAH.

8 AND PLEASE GIVE ME A LETTER ADDRESSED TO ASAPH, THE MANAGER OF THE KING'S FOREST, INSTRUCTING HIM TO GIVE ME TIMBER. I WILL NEED IT TO MAKE BEAMS FOR THE GATES OF THE TEMPLE FORTRESS, FOR THE CITY WALLS, AND FOR A HOUSE FOR MYSELF." AND THE KING GRANTED THESE REQUESTS, BECAUSE THE GRACIOUS HAND OF GOD WAS ON ME.

The king had no reason to suspect Nehemiah of dogging it. Nehemiah must have had a stellar reputation with the king, because he asked for a favor in the context of his reputation as the king's servant. He was not afraid to ask, for he had no need to be ashamed of anything about his service.

It is obvious that Nehemiah had been thinking about what needed to be done. The time of praying, confessing, and fasting had brought him some answers. God had met Nehemiah in his sorrow and begun to give him answers.

Unfortunately, the answer had to do with Nehemiah giving up his luxury, his privilege, and his place. Unfortunately, in a way, God was going to use Nehemiah to answer Nehemiah's prayer — but Nehemiah was ready with the plan and willing with his life.

Leadership must allow the necessary time for the process of recognition, prayer, confession, and consumption to take effect. As we wake up in the middle of the night praying, thinking, and dreaming about our problem, we must ask God what it is we must do. We must be willing to use our assets, lose our comfort, give up our wages, or do whatever is necessary to right the wrong. We will be free when we have no human constraints, no circumstance that prevents us from total dependence and obedience.

Nehemiah was willing to share all that he had, to give up all that made him comfortable, and to risk his very life. Leadership today should desire no less.

Thought for Day 6

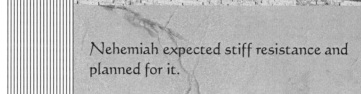

Nehemiah expected stiff resistance and planned for it.

NEHEMIAH 2:9–10 (NLT)

9 WHEN I CAME TO THE GOVERNORS OF THE PROVINCE WEST OF THE EUPHRATES RIVER, I DELIVERED THE KING'S LETTERS TO THEM. THE KING, I SHOULD ADD, HAD SENT ALONG ARMY OFFICERS AND HORSEMEN TO PROTECT ME.

10 BUT WHEN SANBALLAT THE HORONITE AND TOBIAH THE AMMONITE OFFICIAL HEARD OF MY ARRIVAL, THEY WERE VERY DISPLEASED THAT SOMEONE HAD COME TO HELP THE PEOPLE OF ISRAEL.

Nehemiah knew that if this was a good work, a work of Almighty God against the evil one, there would be dogged and determined resistance, and he prepared for it.

Leaders today must realize the same. If we are truly in the middle of the war, we will see battle. If we are actually making progress, we will see increased resistance. If we are making spiritual headway, we will see spiritual casualties.

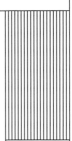

We should not have a depressive, "Eeyore" type of attitude about this, but must prepare—mentally, physically, and spiritually—to do battle. I am afraid that many Christian leaders today are a mile wide and an inch deep. They have been so busy with the administration of God's work that the depth resulting from intimacy with God is nonexistent. Eloquent words, masterful debate, and brilliant rhetoric have replaced truth and intimacy with God.

Throughout the Bible, we see that those who do good pay for it. Jesus warned us about such happenings, and every story of do-gooders in the Bible gives us reason to expect that resistance will be abundant. Jesus heals a lame man, and the religious people start to talk about killing Him. He raises someone from the dead, and they talk about killing Him. The disciples eventually live for Him, and they are killed. Stephen talks as God directs, and he is killed.

Leaders need not fear the battle, the resistance, and the continual fight, but they do need to prepare for it. We need to charge forward knowing that if we are stepping into the evil one's territory, we will be resisted. We must not be surprised by this. We must not pray that the resistance will not be there, because a lack of resistance means that the work we are involved in is irrelevant. We must not judge our work by the lack of problems or resistance we encounter, or by any circumstances that falsely give us a belief that God is blessing us, when in reality God has abandoned us because we withdrew from the field of battle.

Thought for Day 7

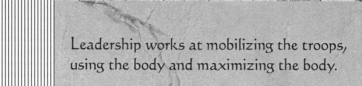

Leadership works at mobilizing the troops,
using the body and maximizing the body.

Nehemiah 3:1–5 (NLT)

1 Then Eliashib the high priest and the other
priests started to rebuild at the Sheep Gate. They
dedicated it and set up its doors, building the wall
as far as the Tower of the Hundred, which they
dedicated, and the Tower of Hananel.

2 People from the town of Jericho worked next to
them, and beyond them was Zaccur son of Imri.

3 The Fish Gate was built by the sons of Hassenaah.
They laid the beams, set up its doors, and installed
its bolts and bars.

4 Meremoth son of Uriah and grandson of Hakkoz
repaired the next section of wall. Beside him
were Meshullam son of Berekiah and grandson
of Meshezabel, and then Zadok son of Baana.

5 Next were the people from Tekoa, though their
leaders refused to work with the construction
supervisors.

Nehemiah was the leader, but he could not accomplish such a huge task on his own—and he knew it. Somehow, he was able to gather the people and give them a vision of what could be and then give them ownership of at least a piece of the whole project.

Often it seems that the art of delegation in Christian leadership is all but dead. Pastors of small churches often end up being pastors, counselors, administrators, janitors, and everything else as well. The people are merely consumers; the professional ministry team has to do it all.

Nehemiah got the people involved. He must have insisted on it; without his insistence, I wonder if the job would have gotten done. At times, leaders need to spend their capital on empowering their people and getting out of the way. Methods are not sacred; principles are sacred, and it is a wise leader who knows the difference, who knows when to step in and correct and when to get out of the way and allow ownership and enthusiasm to continue.

Moses learned this lesson from his father-in-law. He could not do it all, he could not even do a lot of it. The body-of-Christ principle is clear and should be applied by both followers and leaders.

This does not negate the leader's responsibility to lead, but it removes the burden of carrying an unmanageable load.

Thought for Day 8

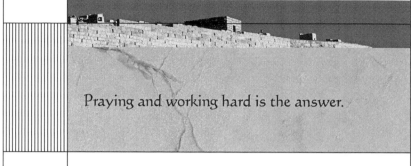

Praying and working hard is the answer.

Nehemiah 4:1–6 (NLT)

1 Sanballat was very angry when he learned that we were rebuilding the wall. He flew into a rage and mocked the Jews,

2 Saying in front of his friends and the Samarian army officers, "What does this bunch of poor, feeble Jews think they're doing? Do they think they can build the wall in a single day by just offering a few sacrifices? Do they actually think they can make something of stones from a rubbish heap—and charred ones at that?"

3 Tobiah the Ammonite, who was standing beside him, remarked, "That stone wall would collapse if even a fox walked along the top of it!"

4 Then I prayed, "Hear us, our God, for we are being mocked. May their scoffing fall back on their own heads, and may they themselves become captives in a foreign land!

5 Do not ignore their guilt. Do not blot out their sins, for they have provoked you to anger here in front of the builders."

6 At last the wall was completed to half its height around the entire city, for the people had worked with enthusiasm.

Opposition to God's work *will* happen. In fact, it will grow no matter what we do to stop it. Nehemiah had a patter here that is worthy of note. When the organized opposition came at him, he prayed hard and worked hard.

Nehemiah demonstrated that his dependence was indeed on God. He did not fight those who opposed him; instead, he prayed and asked God to fight for him. He did not waste his precious assets, but committed his way to God and rolled up his sleeves.

He not only worked hard, he expected his people to work hard. This is different from most ministries today, in that we expect our people to work only if and when it is convenient for them. If it is too much to ask you to adjust your television viewing habits, or too much to ask you to adjust your supper schedule in order to meet the challenges of ministry, the job probably will not be accomplished. It seems that many of today's church leaders want to make it easy to serve, and would never expect someone to actually change his or her personal life so that ministry objectives can be met.

This is a terrible thing, because it causes the people to focus on self, comfort, and personal gain. Our people should be encouraged to pray and work instead of consuming a ministry of convenience.

What the leader expects usually happens. What do you expect?

BEYOND THE RESISTANCE: Learning to Face Adversity

Thought for Day 9

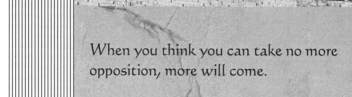

When you think you can take no more opposition, more will come.

NEHEMIAH 4:7 (NLT)

7 BUT WHEN SANBALLAT AND TOBIAH AND THE ARABS, AMMONITES, AND ASHDODITES HEARD THAT THE WORK WAS GOING AHEAD AND THAT THE GAPS IN THE WALL OF JERUSALEM WERE BEING REPAIRED, THEY WERE FURIOUS.

What should we expect?

Should we give up now? Should we adjust because we have offended someone? Should we show more love to Sanballat and Tobiah? Should we be more accommodating to these men and the world around us?

How will they know that we are Christians if we do not love and accept and listen to their woes?

The fact is and will remain that we will face increasing hatred and resistance as we make progress. We must prepare our people for such times.

This seems like a familiar theme, one that should not have to be continuously repeated, yet I am repeating it. Americans need to realize that it is not comfort, wealth, or smooth sailing that makes a difference in our country; it is skillful spiritual warriors who are leading their soldiers into real battle. We need to be continually reminded not to take the easy road, not to give in to the seductions of comfort, not to evaluate our success by peace and prosperity.

Ephesians 6:10–13 (NLT)

10 A final word: Be strong in the Lord and in his mighty power.

11 Put on all of God's armor so that you will be able to stand firm against all strategies of the devil.

12 For we are not fighting against flesh-and-blood enemies, but against evil rulers and authorities of the unseen world, against mighty powers in this dark world, and against evil spirits in the heavenly places.

13 Therefore, put on every piece of God's armor so you will be able to resist the enemy in the time of evil. Then after the battle you will still be standing firm.

When you think you can take no more, more will come. It is not about me; it is not my battle. I need to stand firm. I need to help my people see what this battle is really about.

BEYOND THE RESISTANCE: Learning to Face Adversity

Thought for Day 10

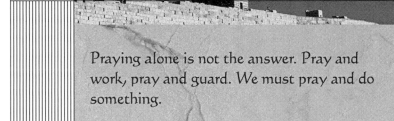

Praying alone is not the answer. Pray and work, pray and guard. We must pray and do something.

NEHEMIAH 4:8–9 (NLT)

8 THEY ALL MADE PLANS TO COME AND FIGHT AGAINST JERUSALEM AND THROW US INTO CONFUSION.

9 BUT WE PRAYED TO OUR GOD AND GUARDED THE CITY DAY AND NIGHT TO PROTECT OURSELVES.

Sometimes I do wish it were easier. Sometimes I wish it were all about my prayer and not about my obedience.

God expects both.

I need to know and truly understand that prayer without action is like trying to exercise without moving. It just does not work.

If I am burdened with something, I should indeed pray, but in addition to prayer, I need to be actively and continuously working on my part of the job. This, again, is beginning to sound rather redundant, but that's the way it is.

The themes in the Bible are not new. They repeat themselves over and over again. Why? Because I have a tendency to forget what was said, not only what was said ten years ago, but what was said ten minutes ago. Reminders are good.

"Let go and let God" sounds good, even spiritual, but it would not have built the wall. "Let go and let God" will probably not feed starving children. Letting go and letting God will probably not erase the hostility in the Middle East. Letting go and letting God will probably not solve your relationship problems. Letting go and letting God will probably not help the needy widow.

I am not trying to negate the fact that we need to do things God's way. If letting go and letting God means letting go of my comfort, my pride, my way, my securities, and so on, I would agree. But letting go and letting God do something that He planned for us to do? No way.

In stage one of this project, there was prayer, confession, and planning. In stage two, there was prayer and the asking of those in power for the necessary resources. In stage three, there was prayer and the giving up of personal comfort. In stage four, there was prayer and empowerment. In stage five, there is prayer and . . . .

There is indeed a pattern here: Prayer *and* something. It is expected, until this wall is finished, that there will be prayer and something. It is expected, when the wall is finished, that there will be prayer and something to maintain the ground gained. In what stage is the ministry in which I serve? Prayer and . . . .

BEYOND THE RESISTANCE: Learning to Face Adversity

Thought for Day 11

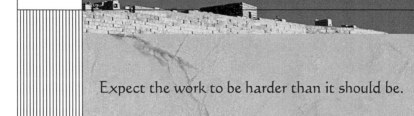

Expect the work to be harder than it should be.

NEHEMIAH 4:12–13 (NLT)

12 THE JEWS WHO LIVED NEAR THE ENEMY CAME AND TOLD US AGAIN AND AGAIN, "THEY WILL COME FROM ALL DIRECTIONS AND ATTACK US!"

13 SO I PLACED ARMED GUARDS BEHIND THE LOWEST PARTS OF THE WALL IN THE EXPOSED AREAS. I STATIONED THE PEOPLE TO STAND GUARD BY FAMILIES, ARMED WITH SWORDS, SPEARS, AND BOWS.

It always seems that the work of God is harder than it should be.

It seems to me that those who serve in the secular world have it easy. Their vehicles run, they know who is in charge in their workplace, they know how many hours they have to work before they go home.

After directing a camp for 25 years, I have found that anything that can go wrong usually does. We could have—and have had—one of the best possible mechanics available, but this is no guarantee that the vehicle will operate correctly when needed. We could budget our resources, hold strictly to the budget, and still have a slew of unexpected expenses. It just always seems that it is harder than it should be.

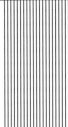

I would like to think that we are the exception on this, but as we see in the book of Nehemiah, we are not. It does not seem right that Nehemiah and his people had to work so hard. Why couldn't God just stop their enemies? Why not make it easy? Why not send angels to repair the wall? Why do these poor people have to post guards and thus substantially reduce the amount of work that can be accomplished?

Because that is the way spiritual warfare is. It is real. It is brutal. Often the work is slowed and greatly hampered.

I need to be prepared for this. I need to prepare my people for this. This should not be a source of discouragement, but a confirmation that we are indeed in the right mine field.

Romans 1:13 (NLT)

13 I WANT YOU TO KNOW, DEAR BROTHERS AND SISTERS, THAT I PLANNED MANY TIMES TO VISIT YOU, BUT I WAS PREVENTED UNTIL NOW. I WANT TO WORK AMONG YOU AND SEE SPIRITUAL FRUIT, JUST AS I HAVE SEEN AMONG OTHER GENTILES.

---

1 Thessalonians 2:18 (NLT)

18 WE WANTED VERY MUCH TO COME TO YOU, AND I, PAUL, TRIED AGAIN AND AGAIN, BUT SATAN PREVENTED US.

It will be harder than it should be. Be prepared.

Thought for Day 12

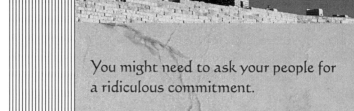

You might need to ask your people for a ridiculous commitment.

NEHEMIAH 4:21 (NLT)

21 WE WORKED EARLY AND LATE, FROM SUNRISE TO SUNSET. AND HALF THE MEN WERE ALWAYS ON GUARD.

Who would think you could ask for such a commitment from your people? Who would think it would be even close to acceptable to ask people to work from sunup to sundown on a ministry-related project?

Perhaps we have not informed our people of the stakes. Perhaps we and our people are too much part of this world. Perhaps we do not know what really matters in life, and are evaluating our lives based on what matters to us but not on what matters to God.

How our people work, not how they talk, gives a good indication of what they think the battle is all about. If they are consumed with reasonableness, then the enemy has the ammunition he needs.

It may be unreasonable to ask our people to give until it hurts, to work long hours, and to give up personal gain for a while. It may be unreasonable because our leadership has not done so. It may be unreasonable because our evaluations have come to be based on the same values by which the secular world evaluates things.

Paul prays that the people in Phillipi will actually know what is important.

Philippians 1:10 (NLT)

10 For I want you to understand what really matters, so that you may live pure and blameless lives until the day of Christ's return.

If it really matters, we put in a "ridiculous" effort. If it really matters, we make no apologies for asking others to follow us and make this same commitment. If it really matters, we will need this type of focus, this type of attitude, and this type of energy to accomplish the goal.

It really mattered that the wall be rebuilt, and that the good name of God be restored. Nehemiah believed this, so he gave up everything to accomplish it. Everyone knew what Nehemiah could have been doing, what he could have had, but he was their leader and he chose to lead rather than just bark orders.

When it comes to spiritual warfare, a ridiculous commitment is the only commitment that counts and the only commitment that works.

Beyond the Resistance: Learning to Face Adversity

Thought for Day 13

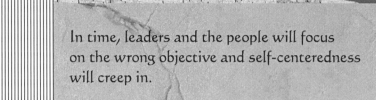

In time, leaders and the people will focus on the wrong objective and self-centeredness will creep in.

Nehemiah 5:1–5 (NLT)

1 About this time some of the men and their wives raised a cry of protest against their fellow Jews.

2 They were saying, "We have such large families. We need more food to survive."

3 Others said, "We have mortgaged our fields, vineyards, and homes to get food during the famine."

4 And others said, "We have had to borrow money on our fields and vineyards to pay our taxes.

5 We belong to the same family as those who are wealthy, and our children are just like theirs. Yet we must sell our children into slavery just to get enough money to live. We have already sold some of our daughters, and we are helpless to do anything about it, for our fields and vineyards are already mortgaged to others."

The leaders had a chance here to help make the people successful. Instead, they used their leadership positions and the assets of leadership for personal gain. While asking the people to give their all, and even demanding that they do so, the leaders were lining their own pockets with excessive and usurious fees. Somewhere, somehow, the leaders found a way to advance their own causes.

Leadership is all about the people, not about us. Leadership involves thinking about and doing whatever it takes to make those around you successful. It is not about doing whatever it takes to make yourself and your family more comfortable.

Jesus made it clear to his disciples that the ultimate leader is one with God in thought and action. He made it clear that if they wanted to be disciples, they must take up their crosses daily. Jesus gave us the ultimate example of giving up all and expecting nothing in return. He washed the disciples' feet and instructed them to follow his lead. He came to be the servant King for the people.

As a leader, I should be no different. If we are going to see God's cause advanced, we are going to have to lead in such a way that the leaders are satisfied only when the people are empowered and the goal is accomplished—even if that means no measurable, personal gain, or even if there is a personal cost.

Thought for Day 14

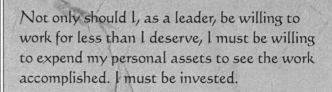

Not only should I, as a leader, be willing to work for less than I deserve, I must be willing to expend my personal assets to see the work accomplished. I must be invested.

NEHEMIAH 6:14 (NLT)

14 REMEMBER, O MY GOD, ALL THE EVIL THINGS THAT TOBIAH AND SANBALLAT HAVE DONE. AND REMEMBER NOADIAH THE PROPHET AND ALL THE PROPHETS LIKE HER WHO HAVE TRIED TO INTIMIDATE ME.

NEHEMIAH 4:18–19 (NLT)

18 ALL THE BUILDERS HAD A SWORD BELTED TO THEIR SIDE. THE TRUMPETER STAYED WITH ME TO SOUND THE ALARM.

19 THEN I EXPLAINED TO THE NOBLES AND OFFICIALS AND ALL THE PEOPLE, "THE WORK IS VERY SPREAD OUT, AND WE ARE WIDELY SEPARATED FROM EACH OTHER ALONG THE WALL."

Nehemiah did not ignore the needs of the people whom he asked to work. In fact, he not only did not ignore them, he used his personal assets to meet their needs.

How important is it for me to accomplish the goal God has placed before my ministry? What am I willing to give, not only in future assets that do not come my way because of my involvement, but also in saved assets that were put away for a rainy day?

It almost seems unreasonable to me that I should consider both working and paying for the work of God. Yet why should that seem unreasonable? It is not my money that I trust. It is not my resources that keep me well fed and healthy. I do actually trust in God, don't I?

This is a most difficult point for me. I seem to expect that those whom I serve should take care of me. I can find references in the Bible to this effect: I, as a leader, am supposed to be free to serve and have my needs met.

This is true. Yet when that does not happen, what does happen? When other resources are not there, but I have some, what do I do? How important is the work I have been called to? Do I see this work as a way to make a living rather than invest my life?

It is easy to accept others' sacrificial gifts on behalf of the work of God. It is good to give out of my abundance to make sure I do not sacrifice too much or disproportionately.

Sorry leaders do not lead with their assets; instead, they demand sacrifices from others.

Thought for Day 15

We must always maintain a "fear" of God.

NEHEMIAH 5:15–16 (NLT)

15 THE FORMER GOVERNORS, IN CONTRAST, HAD LAID HEAVY BURDENS ON THE PEOPLE, DEMANDING A DAILY RATION OF FOOD AND WINE, BESIDES FORTY PIECES OF SILVER. EVEN THEIR ASSISTANTS TOOK ADVANTAGE OF THE PEOPLE. BUT BECAUSE I FEARED GOD, I DID NOT ACT THAT WAY.

16 I ALSO DEVOTED MYSELF TO WORKING ON THE WALL AND REFUSED TO ACQUIRE ANY LAND. AND I REQUIRED ALL MY SERVANTS TO SPEND TIME WORKING ON THE WALL.

We are told that the beginning of wisdom is the fear of God.

PROVERBS 1:7 (NLT)

7 FEAR OF THE LORD IS THE FOUNDATION OF TRUE KNOWLEDGE, BUT FOOLS DESPISE WISDOM AND DISCIPLINE.

Satan knows that if I continue to really fear God, my actions will show that I fear God. It is not man that we should fear, it is not circumstances that we should fear: it is God that we should fear.

God is the creator and sustainer of all things. It is God that has the heart of the king in His hand and like rivers of water moves wherever He pleases. There is no king, no army, no circumstance, no plan that can succeed against God. He will win in the end and all those who obeyed Him will stand with Him victorious.

In the process of building ministry, we can so easily begin to fear the wrong things. We become respecters of persons of means. We become respecters of plans. We begin to entertain pragmatic philosophies that are judged successful just because they seem to work.

We begin to read the newspaper clippings about us. We begin to think outside the realm of warfare, longing for a peace on earth, and will accept almost any compromise to attain this peace.

Nehemiah understood that he needed to maintain his fear of God and that this fear of God would lead him correctly. Leaders today need to spend time being intimate with God. They need to adjust their lives so that they have an abundant amount of time to be in the quiet presence of God. They need to keep renewing the thoughts of God's immensity and His provision, His grace, and His mercy.

They need to keep seeing the job as possible only if God intervenes and only if it is done His way.

BEYOND THE RESISTANCE: Learning to Face Adversity

Thought for Day 16

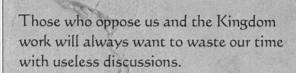

Those who oppose us and the Kingdom work will always want to waste our time with useless discussions.

NEHEMIAH 6:1–3 (NLT)

1 SANBALLAT, TOBIAH, GESHEM THE ARAB, AND THE REST OF OUR ENEMIES FOUND OUT THAT I HAD FINISHED REBUILDING THE WALL AND THAT NO GAPS REMAINED— THOUGH WE HAD NOT YET SET UP THE DOORS IN THE GATES.

2 SO SANBALLAT AND GESHEM SENT A MESSAGE ASKING ME TO MEET THEM AT ONE OF THE VILLAGES IN THE PLAIN OF ONO. BUT I REALIZED THEY WERE PLOTTING TO HARM ME,

3 SO I REPLIED BY SENDING THIS MESSAGE TO THEM: "I AM ENGAGED IN A GREAT WORK, SO I CAN'T COME. WHY SHOULD I STOP WORKING TO COME AND MEET WITH YOU?"

Satan always tries to disrupt us in ways that we would find acceptable. In this case, those who were controlled by Satan wanted Nehemiah to stop his work and come enter into negotiations with them. This sounds good and rational; it sounds like a good activity for the leader of a work to do. In fact, I am certain that no one would have blamed Nehemiah for trying to talk sense to his enemies.

Fortunately, Nehemiah actually knew what he was about. He was not about talk. He was not about making peace with the enemy. He was not about sophisticated negotiations. He was not about political rhetoric. He was about building a wall, and the wall that he was building was a great work that demanded all his energy.

Should you become involved in a great work, there will be many opportunities for you to be intrigued by something or someone that would divert energies and resources to nonessentials.

During World War II, the entire nation needed to focus on winning the war. Fuel was rationed, food was limited, workplaces changed over to wartime uses. The entire nation was focused on the war effort. Nehemiah, the leader, was focused. Those on the outside who wanted to talk could talk, but he was not going to participate with them.

People only have so much energy and so many resources. Once you use up 100 percent, it is all gone. The project that God has called you to, if it is truly of God, will demand your complete allegiance and effort. Be careful not to give in to the vain imaginations of those who know nothing of the real war.

BEYOND THE RESISTANCE: Learning to Face Adversity

Thought for Day 17

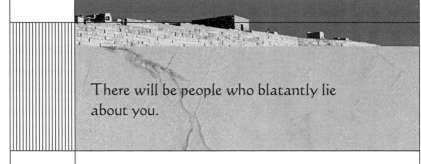

There will be people who blatantly lie
about you.

Nehemiah 6:4–8 (NLT)

4 Four times they sent the same message, and each
time I gave the same reply.

5 The fifth time, Sanballat's servant came with
an open letter in his hand,

6 and this is what it said: "There is a rumor among
the surrounding nations, and Geshem tells me
it is true, that you and the Jews are planning to
rebel and that is why you are building the wall.
According to his reports, you plan to be their king.

7 He also reports that you have appointed prophets
in Jerusalem to proclaim about you, 'Look! There
is a king in Judah!' You can be very sure that this
report will get back to the king, so I suggest that
you come and talk it over with me."

8 I replied, "There is no truth in any part of your
story. You are making up the whole thing."

If you get an open letter with your name on the front and marked "personal," the chances of it really being personal are slim to none. Most likely, everyone whose hands the letter went through read its contents and has begun formulating opinions about you based on lies and innuendo.

If it is not a letter you need to deal with, it will be gossip. If not gossip in the formal sense, you may be prayed about. If it is not from a direct source, it will come from those who have no idea who you are.

You can spend your time, energy, and resources battling the innuendoes, or you can trust that God will take care of justice and wait for Him to do so.

While you wait for God, you must keep working.

I call this type of energy or resource drain *horizontal energy*. This is energy that is just wasted. In the end, when it is all over, nothing was accomplished by the expenditure. The time you put into it is gone. Time that could have been put into the actual war effort was not, and the advancement of the Kingdom was thereby slowed or even stopped.

Your reputation is not that important. If you are doing a great work, keep doing it. Someday your reputation will be restored. Someday, if you indeed are about your Father's business, you will be exonerated.

Jesus was totally misunderstood while on earth. The crowds crucified him. The day of His death appeared to bring shame and disgrace to Him, His family, and His followers. Yet in the end the whole world will acknowledge that He is God.

He is our greatest example.

Thought for Day 18

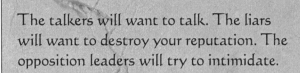

The talkers will want to talk. The liars will want to destroy your reputation. The opposition leaders will try to intimidate.

NEHEMIAH 6:10–14 (NLT)

10 Later I went to visit Shemaiah son of Delaiah and grandson of Mehetabel, who was confined to his home. He said, "Let us meet together inside the Temple of God and bolt the doors shut. Your enemies are coming to kill you tonight."

11 But I replied, "Should someone in my position run from danger? Should someone in my position enter the Temple to save his life? No, I won't do it!"

12 I realized that God had not spoken to him, but that he had uttered this prophecy against me because Tobiah and Sanballat had hired him.

13 They were hoping to intimidate me and make me sin. Then they would be able to accuse and discredit me.

14 Remember, O my God, all the evil things that Tobiah and Sanballat have done. And remember Noadiah the prophet and all the prophets like her who have tried to intimidate me.

You would think that after all this trouble, God would just strike down Nehemiah's enemies with lightning or something. You would think that by now, God would make it easy, since Nehemiah had proven himself over and over again. You would think there would be a time when we have done enough, when God calls off the dogs.

That's what I would think—but the story of Nehemiah indicates that my thinking is incorrect. In fact, the more focused Nehemiah is, the more fiercely the opposition attacks. The more vertical energy we spend, the more horizontal opportunities arise.

If the intrigue and innuendo do not divert you, then certainly outright intimidation must!

Unless, that is, you are one who fears God and nothing or nobody else.

I may never know if I truly fear God until I am placed in a situation where I must choose between the fear of man and the fear of God. I can talk a good talk, but when actual danger comes knocking on my door, what do I do? When the theory of danger turns into the reality of danger, what will I do? When the message that God has placed on my heart goes directly against what the people want and they threaten to undo me, what will be my course of action?

If you are about to embark on a great work, and you are privileged enough to see it through to its completion, it will not be done without many opportunities for a "fear check." Make certain, as best you can, even before you embark, that you actually fear the right person, for when you begin to fear man more than you fear God, you have disqualified yourself from leadership.

Thought for Day 19

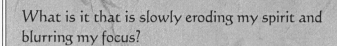

What is it that is slowly eroding my spirit and blurring my focus?

Intrigue, innuendo, and intimidation are insufficient to terrify and drive backward the soldier of the Cross, clad in the armor of righteousness (Eph. 6:10–18); so insinuation is substituted by the insistent and insatiable Adversary of our soul (V. Raymond Edman, *The Disciplines of Life* (Van Kampan Press, 1948), p. 22).

NEHEMIAH 6:17–19 (NLT)

17 DURING THOSE FIFTY-TWO DAYS, MANY LETTERS WENT BACK AND FORTH BETWEEN TOBIAH AND THE NOBLES OF JUDAH.

18 FOR MANY IN JUDAH HAD SWORN ALLEGIANCE TO HIM BECAUSE HIS FATHER-IN-LAW WAS SHECANIAH SON OF ARAH, AND HIS SON JEHOHANAN WAS MARRIED TO THE DAUGHTER OF MESHULLAM SON OF BEREKIAH.

19 THEY KEPT TELLING ME ABOUT TOBIAH'S GOOD DEEDS, AND THEN THEY TOLD HIM EVERYTHING I SAID. AND TOBIAH KEPT SENDING THREATENING LETTERS TO INTIMIDATE ME.

During a fifty-two-day period, many letters came that were intended to instill fear in Nehemiah.

This was a waste of Satan's time.

V. Raymond Edman once said:

*One of the deepest testings of a true child of God is to
stick to his divinely appointed duty when all the while
there is a barrage of letters about him. Intrigue, innuendo,
intimidation, insinuation, these constitute the discipline of
danger. Our temptation is to turn from our task to untangle
the intrigue, to take time to undo the innuendo, to flee
from the intimidation and to fight the hidden insinuation.
Our safety is in doing our duty (2:3), in putting our trust
in God (6:9), in standing steadfast and immovable (6:11),
and serving in silence. The result for us will be as it was with
Nehemiah, the wall will be finished . . . and our enemies will
be cast down in their own eyes: for they perceived that this
work was wrought of our God (6:15, 6:16). Danger feared
is folly, danger faced is freedom (Edman, p.23).*

Thought for Day 20

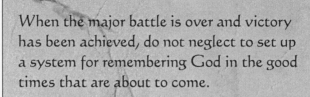

When the major battle is over and victory has been achieved, do not neglect to set up a system for remembering God in the good times that are about to come.

NEHEMIAH 8:1–8 (NLT)

1 ALL THE PEOPLE ASSEMBLED WITH A UNIFIED PURPOSE AT THE SQUARE JUST INSIDE THE WATER GATE. THEY ASKED EZRA THE SCRIBE TO BRING OUT THE BOOK OF THE LAW OF MOSES, WHICH THE LORD HAD GIVEN FOR ISRAEL TO OBEY.

2 SO ON OCTOBER 8 EZRA THE PRIEST BROUGHT THE BOOK OF THE LAW BEFORE THE ASSEMBLY, WHICH INCLUDED THE MEN AND WOMEN AND ALL THE CHILDREN OLD ENOUGH TO UNDERSTAND.

3 HE FACED THE SQUARE JUST INSIDE THE WATER GATE FROM EARLY MORNING UNTIL NOON AND READ ALOUD TO EVERYONE WHO COULD UNDERSTAND. ALL THE PEOPLE LISTENED CLOSELY TO THE BOOK OF THE LAW.

4 EZRA THE SCRIBE STOOD ON A HIGH WOODEN PLATFORM THAT HAD BEEN MADE FOR THE OCCASION. TO HIS RIGHT STOOD MATTITHIAH, SHEMA, ANAIAH, URIAH, HILKIAH, AND MAASEIAH. TO HIS LEFT STOOD PEDAIAH, MISHAEL, MALKIJAH, HASHUM, HASHBADDANAH, ZECHARIAH, AND MESHULLAM.

5 EZRA STOOD ON THE PLATFORM IN FULL VIEW OF ALL THE PEOPLE. WHEN THEY SAW HIM OPEN THE BOOK, THEY ALL ROSE TO THEIR FEET.

6 Then Ezra praised the Lord, the great God, and all the people chanted, "Amen! Amen!" as they lifted their hands. Then they bowed down and worshiped the Lord with their faces to the ground.

7 The Levites—Jeshua, Bani, Sherebiah, Jamin, Akkub, Shabbethai, Hodiah, Maaseiah, Kelita, Azariah, Jozabad, Hanan, and Pelaiah—then instructed the people in the Law while everyone remained in their places.

8 They read from the Book of the Law of God and clearly explained the meaning of what was being read, helping the people understand each passage.

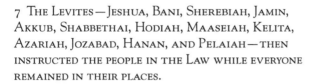

In times of celebration we must not forget our God. We tend to walk closely with God when we "need" Him and we tend to forget Him when all is well.

Upon completion of the project, Nehemiah's people made a deliberate effort to refocus on God, to talk of God in the future and what that would mean to each family. There was one who was teaching who knew the Law of God and knew how to clearly explain its meaning. This teacher helped the people understand each passage.

When the job is complete, the next task is to make sure that our personal and corporate intimacy with God is maintained. It is important that we do not do this with lifeless, uninspired teachers, but turn instead to those who can really communicate and challenge the people. We need to be prepared to turn our people's hearts toward God over and over again.

Should we fail in this task, we will face, in the not-too-distant future, a godless generation that will be worse off than the one we were sent to rescue.

Thought for Day 21

Success with leadership and the people
will always be proportionate to the spiritual
sensitivity of the people.

NEHEMIAH 8:9 (NLT)

9 THEN NEHEMIAH THE GOVERNOR, EZRA THE PRIEST AND
SCRIBE, AND THE LEVITES WHO WERE INTERPRETING FOR
THE PEOPLE SAID TO THEM, "DON'T MOURN OR WEEP ON
SUCH A DAY AS THIS! FOR TODAY IS A SACRED DAY BEFORE
THE LORD YOUR GOD." FOR THE PEOPLE HAD ALL BEEN
WEEPING AS THEY LISTENED TO THE WORDS OF THE LAW.

It seems as though things always come full circle. At the beginning of the book of Nehemiah, Nehemiah was very sensitive to the wrong he was told about. What he heard bothered him to the point of self-sacrificial action.

When the wall had been completed, the people demonstrated a similar mindset. As Ezra read the Law of the Lord, the people wept. They listened to the word of the Lord as it was explained by those who knew it well and examined themselves. This is good and right—but then it was a time for celebration, and the priests and Nehemiah insisted that the people begin to celebrate.

So they did.

There need to be times when we, the soldiers, celebrate. We know that the war will continue. We understand that, in this life, the battles will never be over. Nevertheless, when we see a moment of victory, when we can grasp clearly some newly taken ground, we should also take time to celebrate.

BEYOND THE RESISTANCE: Learning to Face Adversity

Final Thoughts

Nehemiah 8:10–12 (NLT)

10 And Nehemiah continued, "Go and celebrate with a feast of rich foods and sweet drinks, and share gifts of food with people who have nothing prepared. This is a sacred day before our Lord. Don't be dejected and sad, for the joy of the Lord is your strength!"

11 And the Levites, too, quieted the people, telling them, "Hush! Don't weep! For this is a sacred day."

12 So the people went away to eat and drink at a festive meal, to share gifts of food, and to celebrate with great joy because they had heard God's words and understood them.

What a wonderful group of people to work with—at least for now. They actually celebrated with great joy because they had heard God's words and understood them.

That will be the key. Will I be prepared to share God's words, and will those I lead actually understand them? This is what will happen if I am as prepared for the victory as I was for the battle.

The sad reality is that the people of Nehemiah's day soon forgot these wonderful moments. In fact, when Nehemiah went back to visit, he spent most of his time confronting those who had made and then broken promises. There were those who provided Tobiah with a room in the courtyards of the Temple of God; there were those who had begun to work on the Sabbath; there were some men of Judah who had married women of Ashdod, Ammon, and Moab and children who only spoke in the language of Ashdod.

Unfortunately, Nehemiah seemed destined to have a perpetually broken heart, for once again he was called into service to purge out everything foreign, and he assigned tasks to the priests and Levites. Nehemiah once again made sure that the priests and Levites really knew their jobs, and eventually prayed: "Remember this in my favor, O my God."

Nehemiah was a good leader dedicated to the King of Kings. He faced much that could have discouraged him, yet he did not give in.

I pray that the thoughts contained in this booklet will help you think through the tasks that God would have you accomplish, and give you some insight as to how you should approach these tasks.

In the end, God will win. In the end, all will acknowledge Him as God.

May we have the same thought process as Elijah, who asked God to let the world know that God was indeed God and that Elijah was just His servant.

1 Corinthians 15:58 (NLT)

58 So, my dear brothers and sisters, be strong
and immovable. Always work enthusiastically for
the Lord, for you know that nothing you do for
the Lord is ever useless.

Silver Birch Ranch
"To Know Christ and To Make Him Known"

Silver Birch Ranch has been serving our nation's youth since the summer of 1968. Its unique location allows children and families to enjoy swimming, horseback riding, white water rafting and more, while being challenged to understand and respond to God's plan for their lives.

Silver Birch Ranch also hosts year-round conferences and retreats for churches, and a Bible college, the Nicolet Bible Institute.

Silver Birch Ranch has many materials to help you in your effort to be intimate with God and family. Through the *Omega Force* program, you can receive materials that will help you with your personal walk with God, and remind you to live your life with "no regrets."

For information about Silver Birch Ranch, Nicolet Bible Institute, and the Omega Force program, please visit our web site at www.silverbirchranch.org.

If you are interested in inviting Dave Wager as a speaker for your special event, please contact him at Silver Birch Ranch, N6120 Sawyer Lake Road, White Lake, WI 54491, or by email at dave.wager@silverbirchranch.org.

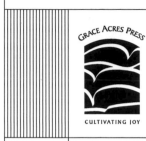

GRACE ACRES PRESS

CULTIVATING JOY

Grace Acres Press products and services bring joy to your heart and life. Visit us at www.GraceAcresPress.com.

Future titles in this series:

Beyond the Compass: Learning to See the Unseen
Beyond the Deception: Learning to Defend the Truth
Beyond the Expected: Learning to Obey
Beyond the Feeling: Learning to Listen

For orders or information about quantity discounts or reprints,
Call 888-700-GRACE (4722)
Fax (303) 681-9996
Email info@GraceAcresPress.com